MONADNOCK TALES

for Nai,
best wishes in your
poetry, a beautiful world!

MONADNOCK TALES

by Edie Clark

Edie Clark

THE BROWN RABBIT PRESS

Peterborough, New Hampshire

First Printing May 2002
Printed in the United States of America
10 9 8 7 6 5 4 3   paperback

ISBN 0-9719934-0-8

ACKNOWLEDGMENTS

The complete work entitled *Monadnock Tales* was the result of a commission
by Tricinium, Ltd., to collaborate with the composer, Larry Siegel, for a
project to celebrate the Monadnock Region. Together, we created a work
entitled *Monadnock Tales,* a fusion of music and poetry. The work's debut
performance was on May 12, 2002, at the Colonial Theater in Keene, New
Hampshire. The music was performed by the Keene Chamber Orchestra
under the direction of Eric Stumacher, with Lewis Feldstein as narrator.
      Grateful acknowledgments are given to the Monadnock Millennium
and to the Putnam Foundation for their generous support of this effort.
The work would not have been possible without their help. Thanks also to
Eric Stumacher, Lew Feldstein, Leigh Marthe, Jill Shaffer, Michael Haman,
Tim Clark, and MaryLou DiPietro.
      The words in the poems printed in this book are slightly different from
those in the symphonic work. Some portions were changed in deference to
the music. These are the complete, unabridged words. A compact disc of the
work will be available soon.

EDITOR'S NOTE: *There are as many views of Monadnock as there are points on
the compass. The rendering featured in this book represents the view from the
author's window.*

Book design by Jill Shaffer
The Brown Rabbit Press
6 Powersbridge Road
Peterborough, New Hampshire 03458

Contents

If a mountain could be
a town,
Mt. Monadnock would be ours,
our center,
our meeting place,
the rising point
that greets our days,
the long black body that
spreads across the starry sky
and guards
our nights.

If that mountain
were a town,
in that town
would live
painters and writers,
farmers and hikers,
dancers and fiddlers,
and
lovers,
their stories
written on the walls.

Great gray granite
blade,
sharpened on sun
and ice.
Enduring presence
on a warring planet,

you were here
long
before us.
You will be here
long
after us.
Mother of lore,
your stories
are told now.

We listen.

Wahmodmaulk

The word itself is
the first story,
the first mystery.

Monadnock,
spoken by Indians
who lived
on the mountain,
a thousand or more in number,
before we came –
Mon
Adn
Ock
they said:
Algonquian words
we made into one.
We find it now in our dictionary,
a word meaning
The mountain that stands alone.
Or does it?
The Abenakis say
it is
Menonadenak
meaning
smooth mountain
or
Menadena
meaning
isolated mountain.

When we write it,
we stumble
on the mystery
of the letters.
The Indians said it,
felt it,
lived it,
but never
spelled it.

We try to explain it.

And for every one who wrote it
in our histories,
the word came out differently:

Manadnuck
Manadnock
Manudnock
Manadnach
Monadnuck
Monadnick
Monodoch
Menadnack
Menadnick
Menorgnuck
Menagnick
Wanadnock
Wenadnock
Wannadnack
Wenadnack
Wahnodnock

Wahmodmaulk

Are we close yet?

Monadnock.

The linguists say
perhaps it means:
Place where is a high mountain.
Or
Land of the surpassing mountain.
Or is that
the *unexcelled* mountain?
Revered mountain.
Lookout mountain.
And then there is
just
Wonderful mountain.

The experts pick over the differences,
looking for
the right words,
the right letters.
How about:
The only mountain
like this
in the world.

We like to think that.

Almost
every other mountain
on earth
is part of a range,
one
among many.

You are your own
or else
the towns that grew up around you
are the other peaks,
in the spreading range
of towns that circle you
like wagons
around a bonfire,
or
like cabins
around a lake:
We all drink from you.

Bountiful Mountain

At first,
you had trees
to the summit,
a bushy top.
Only Bald Rock
stood bare.
Animals grazed
in open fields
below the trees.

Wolves
prowled.

And feasted.

Farmers
wept
for their lost sheep.

The farming was hard enough:
Those steep fields
with all those rocks.
But
to the wolves
they lost their calves
their sheep
their chickens.
We think
Little Red Riding Hood
a quaint tale.

To them,
it was real,
a chaos
that came from
the top
of that great enduring presence
above.

A bounty was offered
on the scalps of the wolves.
In 1793
farmers
like Benjamin Mason and
Reuben Morse
collected eight dollars
for the scalps they turned in.
But their hunting was not enough.
At night
their calves and their sheep
continued
to die.

It was fire
that brought them
down.

The first fire was
in, maybe,
1800.
Was it
summer lightning that
struck
like matches
passed

across a hot
stovetop
or was it
the angry farmers
with their torches?

This we know:
Fires burst,
volcanic tongues,
through the tindery
earth-starved trees
clinging to
your crown.
No one stopped
the racing flames,
a blaze that lit
the mountain
for weeks.

An awful beauty.

One farmer said
at night
he could read
his newspaper
by the light
of the fires
that rippled
across your big spine.

When embers
cooled,
your granite face
emerged,

a full moon
rising
above our days.

It was
the farmers who set
the second fire.
1820, that's our best guess.
Fire flared up out of the thicket,
hot spits
roasting
wolves and cubs
and home.

After that,
the wolves
were gone.

Except for one:
The lone wolf.

He came at night
and continued the kill.
One farmer lost
sixteen
of his flock
in one night
to the appetite
of that
one.

It was winter.
They upped the ante.
Every able-bodied man and boy
and keen-scented hound

from every town
around the mountain
gathered
with their guns:
A wolf militia.

The villagers chased
that elusive warrior
through Jaffrey and Fitzwilliam,
Winchendon and Rindge.
Even,
they say,
down into Templeton and Gardner.

Snows piled deep.
That phantom
was often seen,
and fired at,
dodging,
dashing hopes.

At the bottom
of the mountain,
the farmers banded together
and worked their way
in a chain —
all the way to the top.
All they discovered there
was an old bear and her two cubs.

No wolf.

The men
descended,
discouraged.

All night
they stood guard.
Through darkness
they heard his
bark
like the sound
of an alarm.

At first light,
the ragged army
spotted him
again
and cornered that
lingering veil
of hunger
in a farmer's field
in Fitzwilliam.
Fifty shots
poked the cold
air.
Now but
a haunting shadow,
the cunning thief
vanished
to another meadow
where a young man
hit him square
and proudly
collected the twenty dollars
promised.

No wolf has ever been seen here since.

And sheep still safely graze.

Secret Places

We don't know
the mountain
the way they used to.
Who among us can find
Ballou City?
Who can find the Dingle Dell?
Monte Rosa.
The Sphinx.
Baby Bicknell.

Lost Farm.

Point Surprise.

Who wrote this poem
of secret places?

Men like
Henry MacGowan
And George Noble,
Alfred Wilmot, Scott Smith
and little
Marion Wright,
they wrote this verse
with their axes,
cutting trails
one
at a time,
naming them:

Cart Path
Twisted Birch
Paradise Valley
Inspiration Rock.

We know
the trails
that survived:
Red Dot
and Pumpelly.
Cascade Link
and Birchtoft.
We climb
the ladder of the
White Cross.
When we reach the top,
we eat
granola bars from our backpacks,
sip spring water
from bottles,
and search the horizon
for Boston.

But do we remember,
Dinsmore's Shanty,
where you could,
if you wanted,
buy a glass of whiskey?
Even in 1824,
there was a hotel,
at the very top.
After your vigorous climb,
you could drink and eat hearty
at table
and then sleep

up there
with the stars.

A friend remembers –
not that long ago –
when they hiked
the woman who lived
at The Halfway House
always came out to greet them
with her toy poodles.
She gave them sweaters
to be sure they'd be warm enough
for the climb.
The Halfway House is
gone now – burned
to the ground.
Where did the woman
and her poodles go?
Who gives sweaters to
the climbers now?

But there's so much
more.
If we look closely,
we see the etchings of
ice and thaw,
ice and
thaw.

In winter
so few climb.
Those that do,
resting on snowbanks
and plates
of ice,

might think back –
not to the Halfway House – but
eons
before fires
before wolves
before slippered Indians
made their way.
They might think back
to a great primitive rock,
an Alp,
an Everest,
a heaving, steaming,
fire-breathing peak,
ground down
and washed away
by the great creep
of ice and time.

Our trails are but pencil lines
on an ancient map.
Faint shadows on an old mask.

Monadnock Rap

How do we hear
this name now
that it has
escaped from
from the Indians'
tongues?

We hear it
in our businesses,
a rocking
tune
that starts
slow:

Monadnock Antiques . . .
Monadnock Auto Body . . .
Monadnock Berries . . .

Monadnock Appraisal
Monadnock Disposal

Monadnock Cremation
Monadnock Restoration

Monadnock Construction
Monadnock Rod and Gun

Monadnock Optical
Monadnock Technical

Monadnock Emporium
Monadnock Hemporium

Monadnock Speedway
Monadnock United Way

Monadnock Rental
Monadnock Dental

Monadnock Erectors
Monadnock Fire Protectors

Monadnock View
Monadnock Tatoo

Monadnock Co-op
Monadnock Business Op.

Monadnock Mason-ary
Monadnock Veterinary

Monadnock Healing Arts
Monadnock Performing Arts

Monadnock Music
Monadnock Electric . . .
Orthopedic!
Pediatric!
Orthodontic!
Geriatric!
Psychiatric! . . . Monadnock Septic!!

And we can't forget

The Monadnock
School
For
Natural
Cooking
            And   Philosophy.

Music, Rising

There has always been
music
on the mountain.

There is, first of all,
the music of the mountain itself,
which Thoreau remembered
as the moaning
of wind
over rocks,
a sound, he said,
that made him feel
closer to the moon
than to the plains.

Maybe this was
the roar,
The Monadnock Roar,
which farmers said
came before a storm,
sounding like
a hundred bulls,
surging,
a sound that,
like thunder,
was over in seconds —
and then came the storm.
Who now hears
the mountain roar?
We have to be

quiet
to hear that song.

Men made music
too.
Back in the 1800s,
an old farmer
told
of a group
of young men and women
who
ascended the mountain
all the way to the peak.
On their shoulders,
they carried boards.
When they reached the top,
they made
a level floor
and there
the fiddler began
and they danced.
The farmer knew
because he was already up there,
on top,
and watched the young ones arrive
with their puzzle.
When they'd put
the pieces together,
he danced too.

Not long after,
in 1866,
the members of The Unionville Brass Band
of Swanzey
climbed high with

their trombones
and their tubas
and their coronets
in hand.
The Keene Sentinel made note:
"The first brass band ever
on Monadnock
took their instruments to the tip-top
and there
discoursed
some of their best music."
Ever.

Below,
farmers, in their fields,
might have heard
distant sounds
drifting down,
causing them to stop
and listen
in wonder.
Were the angels
on parade?

In fact,
things happen
on the tip-top.

One thing we know:
Love happens.

On October 2
of that same year,
Luther Richardson
of Stoddard

married
Rachel Tarbox
of Sullivan.
The ceremony was performed
by Reverend Peabody
above the
candy-colored
glory of the
autumn leaves.
So far as is known,
that was the first union
created on the tip-top
of Monadnock.
Even now,
ministers
are known to dread the words:
We want to be married on the top
of the mountain.
But they usually
climb anyway,
hiking boots
beneath their
robes.
And the vows
drift down,
like the best music,
ever.

We dance
there
still
on your solid
peaceful
top.
In September

Diane Eno
and her dancing friends
sprint to the summit
and leap
in joy
from rock to rock.
In April
Ken LaRoche
ascends,
listens
to the music
of the snow
melting
and plays his flute:
"Monadnock Spring."

The shriek
of soaring
hawks;
the pipe
of the ovenbird;
the grouse's thrum
inside a hollow log,
all this
your music
too.
Along the paths,
running
in the streams
and on the
wind,
there will always
be music,
rising.

The Pilgrims' Tales

(Ahem!)
So far as we know,
Captain Samuel Willard
was the first
white man
to climb our peak,
on a July day
in 1725.
The trees
were dense
but he found signs
of Indians
who had camped there
before him.
We can count him,
then,
as our first pilgrim.

Since then
and especially after the fires
extinguished
the wolves,
thousands,
no,
millions
have climbed to the top.
On a good day
now
twelve thousand
can be counted,

touching rock,
gazing sky,
and that means
there are always more
who come on trails
outside the park.
Day after
climbing day,
our booted feet
caress
your sides:
The most climbed mountain
in the world,
they say –
get down,
Mount Fuji!

ოოოო

Larry Davis,
a strong-legged
Jaffrey man,
climbed to the top
every day
two thousand,
eight hundred
and fifty
days in a row.
Like the mailman,
he ran through rain, ice, snow.
Sleet.
Sunshine too.
A very long prayer
to the mountain gods.

"To stay in shape,"
he said
at first.
But then he couldn't stop.
Eight years
climbing,
his footsteps echoing
on the fragrant air.
Not a day missed,
except for three days, one February –
they must have been
bad days.
Very bad days.

Like the Knight and the Miller,
the Squire and the Wife of Bath,
these pilgrims come,
full of homage,
up the White Cross,
the Dot
or Pumpelly,
young people
with packs on their backs,
and old people
with walking sticks.
Little children skip
and sometimes cry.
All celebrants
at the same table,
ordinary people
in sneakers
and fleece
make the trek up
and then down
for dinner at the inn.

Some, though, get lost
or collapse
and surprisingly,
sometimes die.
It's a simple mountain
that can fool.

❧❧❧❧

When Thoreau climbed
he picked blackberries
along the way
and saw a bald eagle
gliding overhead.

In daylight
he took notes on what
he discovered:
Andromeda
Lambkill
Checkerberry
Viburnum
Mountain ash
Potentilla
Black spruce.
And on what he heard:
Nighthawks
Chewinks
Wood thrush.

As well as what he liked,
he noted what he disliked:
Newspapers and eggshells
left by hikers.
And graffiti!

Into the granite
the names
Charlie and Lizzie
had been carved.
Disgusted,
Thoreau wrote:
"Charles carried the sledgehammer
and Lizzie the cold chisel,"
pure surmise
but a clear picture
of these early defacers of our mount.
(Oh, but weren't they lovers, too?)
More to his liking
were the lichens
that decorated the mountain in
"the color of antiquity."

Over time,
our pilgrim Thoreau
roamed the mountain,
gathering blueberries in his hat,
listening to
bullfrogs
and praising
cloud shadows.

At night,
he boiled
rice
beside a rainwater pond,
slept in
a "sunken yard"
and at midnight
he awakened and
strolled across the rocky summit

by moonlight.
One can only imagine
the enormous
sleeping world
he saw
below.

ლოლოლო

Much later and perhaps
even more devoted,
Willa Cather came,
thirty summers
not to Nebraska
(her home)
but to Jaffrey,
mountain gazing.

In a meadow
near the inn
she pitched her tent.
Mornings,
she worked on
My Antonia.
Afternoons,
wildflower book in hand,
she walked up her beloved peak,
imagining Nebraska.

The hurricane
in '38
broke the trees and
her heart.
She never returned
except

to be buried here,
"in sight of the mountain,"
as was her wish.
So few know
her grave is there,
tucked in the corner
of the Meetinghouse yard
And those who do, ask,
Why here?
Her secret.
And ours as well.

పడుపడు

Abbott Thayer,
that famous
Dublin eccentric
who slept
outdoors under
bearskins,
regarded
Monadnock
as totem,
an object
of worship,
which he did,
with his brush,
painting Gabriel's
angels,
their wings eclipsing
the top.
Was the mountain's light
otherwise
too bright?
Did he mean to

protect us
from its light?

൦൦൦൦

Another pilgrim,
William Preston Phelps,
born in sight of Monadnock,
sat through storms
to paint the big hill.
His mecca.

How many canvases?
No one knows.
But they show
snow
and glare ice,
dark skies
and mist,
gathering storms
and the blazing, fiery
leaves of autumn.
In these pictures,
he gave us
not a pretty postcard
but a mirror,
the great tumult
of who we are.

Like Van Gogh,
Phelps painted himself
into the asylum.
In his last years,
everything was gone,

the farm
and all his paintings,
all gone for debts.
He left us beauty
and a gauge.
We see his mountain:
How changed!
What once was gray
is turning green
again.
That big
moon face
shrinking.

Monadnock Return

Each year,
trees creep up
farther toward the peak.
Will there be
again
the bushy top?

And wolves?
A woman
who lives near
the base of the mountain
says
she has seen
a wolf.
A big gray dog,
she reports,
wild and toothy.
When she asks
she is told:
there are no wolves here.

But, listen:
Twenty years ago,
someone thought
they saw
a coyote.
No, no,
they said,
there are no coyotes
here.

Maybe not, then.
But now
coyotes, lots of them,
live
close to the hill.
And at night
or sometimes even
in daylight
they howl,
a looping opera
of hoots
and shrill cries.

David,
our sheep farmer,
watches his flock
and when he can't,
his llama does,
spitting and hissing
at the prowling dogs.
Even so,
David has lost sheep
but the other barns
on the old farms here
are empty of
flocks or herds,
filled instead with
old cars
or boats
or furniture.
No wonder the coyotes
cry.

But
what is a wolf?

Or the growth
of a tree?
When the towers
fell, showering
broken glass
around the world,
we cried
too,
covering
our ears
and hiding our faces.
You stood
still.

Great gray granite
blade,
sharpened on sun
and ice.
Enduring presence
on a warring planet,
you were here
long
before us.
You endure all
change.
Even this.
Even this.

Wonderful Mountain

We want
again
to find your
secret places:
Baby Bicknell,
The Sphinx,
Ballou City,
Point Surprise.
And to count
your
andromeda,
your potentilla,
to listen
to your
nighthawks
beside a rainwater pond.

At the millennium
someone
climbed to your top,
with rockets
in his pockets:
Secret fireworks.
At midnight
faint sparks
lifted
from your peak
like a little
Vesuvius.

In the last war,
you were our
stairway
to the sky.
Up top,
we could have seen
the Germans coming,
if they had,
the shapes of their planes
distinctive.
In this war
when towers
turned to
inferno
we saw nothing
but blue sky
and cloud shadows
crossing your soothing
shape.
We heard nothing
but the terrible
silence
that followed.

We fell
to our knees,
unsteady.
You were
our handrail:
Something to
hold on to.
Something to
help us up.

We have seen
your sides
on fire
and, once,
a plane
crumpled
against your rock.
No earth shook.
No pieces fell.

Your virgin slopes
remain,
green,
target of nothing
but our admiring
eyes.

We are so
grateful.

If a mountain could be
a town,
you would be ours,
our center,
our meeting place,
the rising point
that greets our days.

Smooth mountain.
Isolated mountain.
Mountain that stands
alone.
You are your own.
You are *our* own.

Even with
your changing
face,
you endure
all change.
All change.

We are,
all of us,
pilgrims
in need
of you.

We all drink from you.

And rejoice.

Sources

The Annals of Grand Monadnock by Allen Chamberlain, Society for the Protection of New Hampshire Forests, Concord, NH, 1968.

The Grand Monadnock, A Literary, Artistic and Social History, Society for the Protection of New Hampshire Forests, 1974.

The Grand Monadnock by Albert Annet, Society for the Protection of New Hampshire Forests, 1927.

The Heart of Monadnock by Elizabeth Weston Timlow, B.J. Brimmer Co., Boston, 1922.

Into the Mountains by Maggie Stier, Appalachian Mountain Club, 1995.

Some Painters of Grand Monadnock by Hildreth M. Allison, 1923.

Monadnock Guide, Henry Ives Baldwin, editor, Society for the Protection of New Hampshire Forests, 1970.

To Monadnock by Helen Cushing Nutting, Stratford Press, New York, 1925.

A Circle of Friends: Art Colonies of Cornish and Dublin, University Art Galleries, University of New Hampshire, Durham, N.H., 1985.

The History of Dublin, N.H., Town of Dublin, N.H., 1920.

The History of Dublin, N.H., by Levi Leonard, J. Wilson & Son, 1855.

The History of Fitzwilliam, N.H. by Rev. John Norton, 1888.

Dublin (NH) archives, John Harris, curator.

The Phelps/Hayward papers from the Smithsonian Archives of American Art.

Abbott H. Thayer, Painter and Naturalist by Nelson C. White, Connecticut Printers, Inc., 1951.

The Journal of Henry David Thoreau, B. Torrey and F.H. Allen, editors, Houghton Mifflin Co., Boston, 1906.

Yankee Magazine archives.

About the Artists

EDIE CLARK is an award-winning writer and editor. Her memoir, *The Place He Made,* received national recognition. She lives and works in direct view of Mt. Monadnock.

LARRY SIEGEL is a nationally known figure in community arts and traditional music, as well as a classical composer. His musical, *The People's House,* was produced in Concord last year and received praise from around the state. His music has won many awards. He lives in Westmoreland.

ERIC STUMACHER is the leader of the Keene Chamber Orchestra and the Apple Hill Chamber Players. A resident of Sullivan, Eric is known as a vigorous and thoughtful pianist and conductor. He takes his work around the world with his project, "Playing for Peace," in which musicians from Israel and several Arab countries have performed together.

TRICINIUM, LTD., is a not-for-profit arts presenting and producing organization based in New Hampshire. Their mission is to aid in the development and production of innovative work in the performing arts.